10110

MONTREAL CANADIENS

By Craig Zeichner

The
Child's
World®

THE CHILD'S WORLD®
1980 Lookout Drive • Mankato, MN 56003-1705
800-599-READ • www.childsworld.com

ACKNOWLEDGMENTS
The Child's World®: Mary Berendes, Publishing Director
Shoreline Publishing Group, LLC: James Buckley, Jr.,
 Production Director
The Design Lab: Gregory Lindholm, Design and
 Page Production

PHOTOS
Cover: AP/Wide World
Interior: AP/Wide World: 5, 6, 9, 10, 18, 21, 25 left, 25
 bottom; Getty Images: 13, 17, 22, 25 top right, 26, 27

LIBRARY OF CONGRESS
CATALOGING-IN-PUBLICATION DATA
Zeichner, Craig.
 Montreal Canadiens / by Craig Zeichner.
  p. cm.
 Includes bibliographical references and index.
 ISBN 978-1-60253-440-7 (library bound : alk. paper)
 1. Montreal Canadiens (Hockey team)—History—Juvenile
literature. I. Title.

 GV848.M6Z45 2010
 796.962'640971428—dc22

2010015295

Printed in the United States of America
Mankato, Minnesota
July 2010
F11538

TABLE OF CONTENTS

GO, CANADIENS!

A Canadiens player skates up the ice. His stick pushes the **puck** in front of him. He takes a big swing and the puck flies toward the net. The other team's **goalie** tries to block it with his pads, but misses. The puck smacks into the net for a Canadiens goal! The Canadiens win! The players raise their sticks and celebrate. Let's meet the Montreal Canadiens.

The Montreal Canadiens celebrate another big goal.

6

The great goalie Patrick Roy lifts the Stanley Cup. The Canadiens won the Cup for the 24th time in 1993.

WHO ARE THE MONTREAL CANADIENS?

The Montreal Canadiens play in the National Hockey League (NHL). They are one of 30 teams in the NHL. The NHL includes the Eastern Conference and the Western Conference. The Canadiens play in the Northeast Division of the Eastern Conference. The playoffs end with the winners of the Eastern and Western conferences facing off. The champion wins the **Stanley Cup**. The Canadiens have won 24 Stanley Cups.

WHERE THEY CAME FROM

The Canadiens are the oldest hockey team in the NHL. They first skated in 1909 in a league called the Canadian Hockey Association. They won their first Stanley Cup in 1916—before there even was an NHL! They joined the NHL in 1917. The Canadiens are one of the Original Six—the first teams in the league. They have won 24 Stanley Cups, more than any other NHL team.

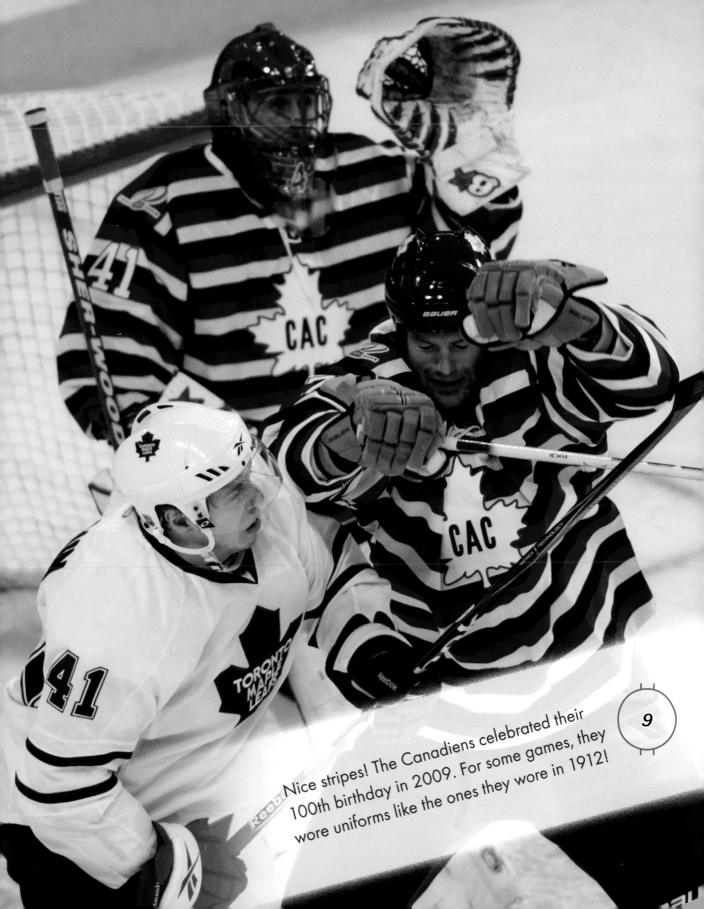

Nice stripes! The Canadiens celebrated their 100th birthday in 2009. For some games, they wore uniforms like the ones they wore in 1912!

It's always a battle when the Canadiens and the Maple Leafs face off.

WHO THEY PLAY

The Montreal Canadiens play 82 games each season. They play all the other teams in their division six times. The other Northeast Division teams are the Boston Bruins, the Buffalo Sabres, the Ottawa Senators, and the Toronto Maple Leafs. The Canadiens are fierce **rivals** of the Bruins and the Maple Leafs. The Canadiens also play other teams in the Eastern and Western Conferences.

11

WHERE THEY PLAY

During the Canadiens' greatest years, they played at the Montreal Forum. Since 1996, the Canadiens have played their home games in the Bell Centre in Montreal. The **arena** is also used for ice shows, basketball, indoor soccer, and concerts. When the arena opened in 1996, it was called the Molson Center.

The Bell Centre was home to the 2009 NHL All-Star Game. A special ceremony was held before the game.

13

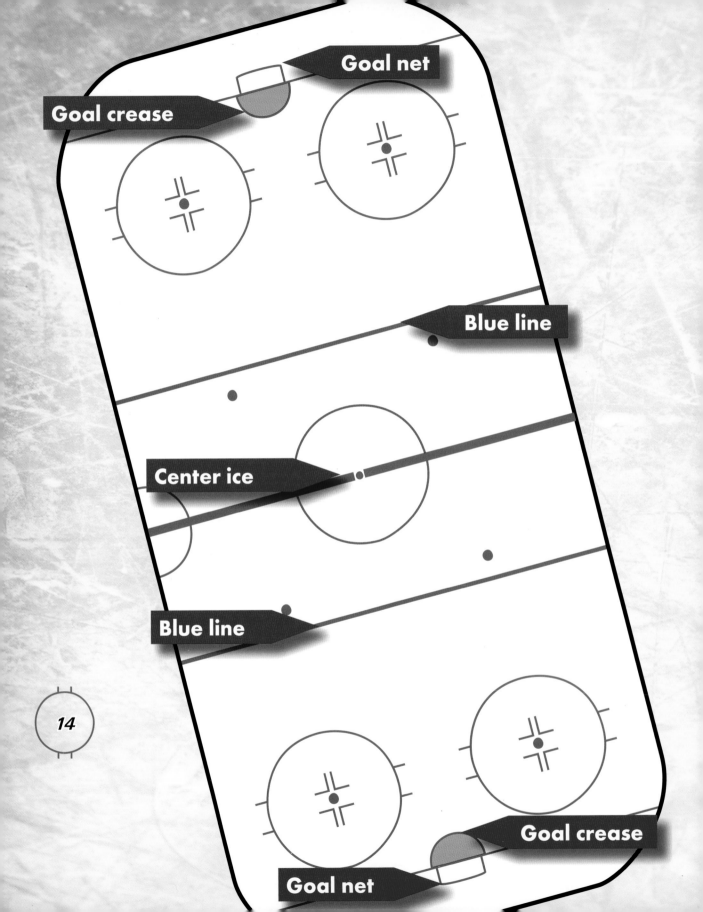

Goal net

Goal crease

Blue line

Center ice

Blue line

Goal crease

Goal net

14

THE HOCKEY RINK

Hockey games are played on a sheet of ice called a rink. It is a rounded rectangle. NHL rinks are 200 feet (61 m) long and 85 feet (26 m) wide. Wooden boards surround the entire rink. Clear plastic panels are on top of the boards so fans can see the action and be protected from flying pucks. Netting is hung above the seats at each end of the rink to catch any wild pucks. The goal nets are near each end of the rink. Each net is four feet (1.2 m) high and six feet (1.8 m) wide. A red line marks the center of the ice. Blue lines mark each team's defensive zone.

THE PUCK

An NHL puck is made of very hard rubber. The disk is three inches (76 mm) wide and 1 inch (25 mm) thick. It weighs about 6 ounces (170 g). It's black so it's easy to see on the ice. Many pucks are used during a game, because some fly into the stands.

BIG DAYS!

The Canadiens have had many great seasons in their long history. Here are three of the greatest.

1915–16: Led by **center** Newsy Lalonde, the Canadiens won their first Stanley Cup championship.

1959–60: The Canadiens won their fifth Stanley Cup in a row! Center Henri Richard and **wing** Bernie Geoffrion had 12 **points** each. The Canadiens did not lose a single game in the playoffs.

1985–86: The Canadiens defeated the Calgary Flames to win their 23rd Stanley Cup. **Rookie** goalie Patrick Roy won the Conn Smythe trophy as the MVP of the playoffs.

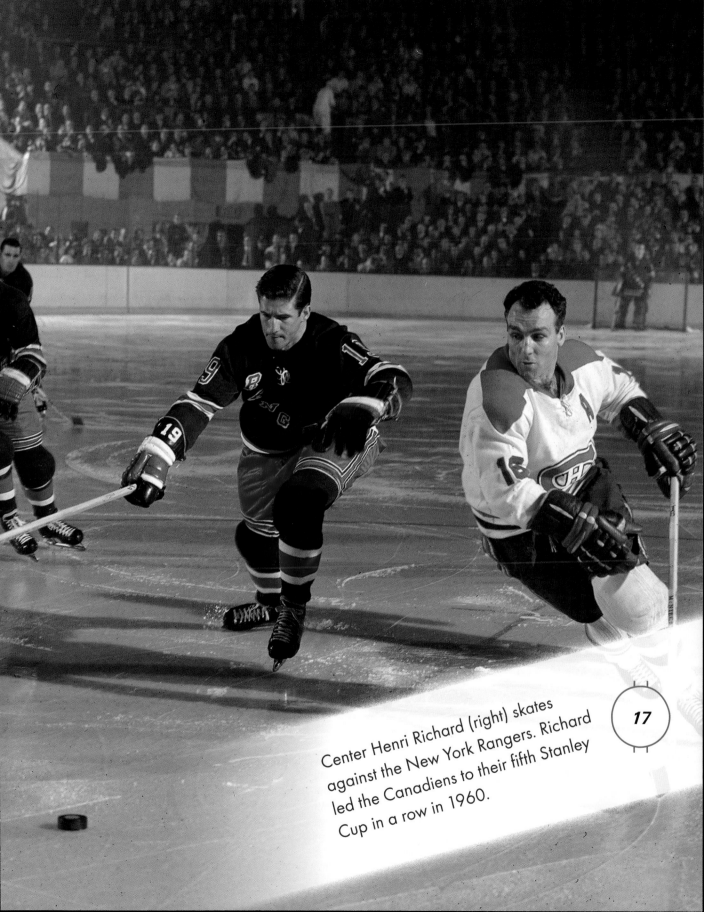

Center Henri Richard (right) skates against the New York Rangers. Richard led the Canadiens to their fifth Stanley Cup in a row in 1960.

Another goal . . . for the wrong team! The Canadiens lost to the Bruins in the 2008 playoffs.

TOUGH DAYS!

Not every season can end with a Stanley Cup championship. Here are some of the toughest seasons in Canadiens history.

1939–40: The Canadiens played 48 games but only won 10! They finished in last place.

1969–70: The Canadiens were expected to win their third Stanley Cup in a row. But they finished in fifth place and did not make the playoffs.

2007–08: The Canadiens had a great season and finished in first place. But they lost to the Boston Bruins in the second round of the playoffs.

MEET THE FANS

Montreal Canadiens fans are crazy about their team! Everywhere you go in Montreal, shops sell Canadiens **sweaters** and hats. Because many Canadiens fans speak French, they sometimes call the team by their nickname "le bleu, blanc et rouge" (LEH BLUH, BLAHNK AY ROOZH) This is French for "the blue, white, and red," which are the colors of the Canadiens sweaters. The fans like to cheer in French, too. They shout "but!" (BOOT) when a Canadien puts the puck into the net. This means "goal!" Canadiens fans also sing "Ole, ole, ole, ole" when the Canadiens score a goal.

This Canadiens fan painted his face with the team's colors. The "CH" stands for the French words for "Club Hockey."

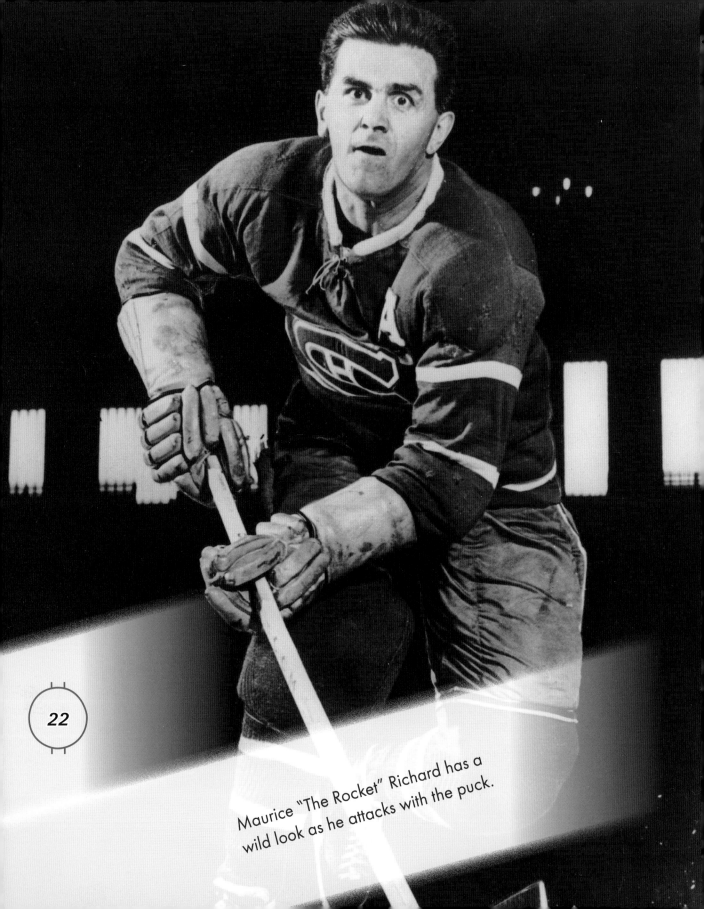

Maurice "The Rocket" Richard has a wild look as he attacks with the puck.

HEROES THEN...

There are many Canadiens in the **Hockey Hall of Fame**. Wing Maurice Richard was one of the most dangerous goal-scorers ever. He was the first NHL player to score 50 goals in a season. His 544 goals are the most in Canadiens history. His nickname was "The Rocket." Center Henri Richard was Maurice's brother. Henri won 11 Stanley Cups—the most of any player in NHL history. **Defenseman** Larry Robinson was tall, tough, and strong. He was the player who guarded the other teams' best scorers. Wing Guy Lafleur has 1,246 points, the most in Canadiens history. Goalie Jacques Plante has the most wins by a Canadiens goalie, with 314. He was also the first goalie to wear a face mask.

HEROES NOW...

The Canadiens have some of the top players in the NHL. Wing Michael Camalleri is a speedy skater and a dangerous goal-scorer. Center Tomas Plekanec is known for passing the puck. Plekanec is also great at stealing the puck from the other team and then scoring a goal. Defenseman Andrei Markov is one of the best players at controlling the puck. Markov played in the 2008 All-Star game. Wing Brian Gionta is a small, skilled player. Andrei Kostitsyn is a hard-hitting wing who can also score goals. His brother Sergei also plays for the Canadiens.

WING

MICHAEL CAMALLERI

WING

BRIAN GIONTA

CENTER

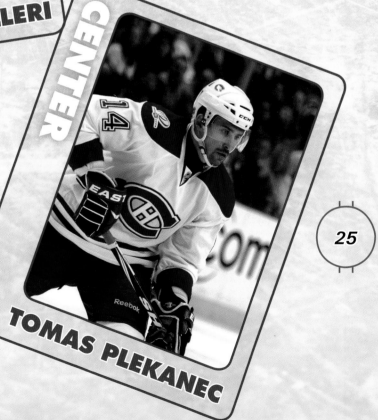

TOMAS PLEKANEC

GEARING UP

Hockey players wear short pants and a jersey called a "sweater." Underneath, they wear lots of pads to protect themselves. They also wear padded gloves and a hard plastic helmet. They wear special ice hockey skates with razor-sharp blades. They carry a stick to handle the puck.

Goalies wear special gloves to help them block and catch shots. They have extra padding on their legs, chest, and arms. They also wear special decorated helmets and use a larger stick.

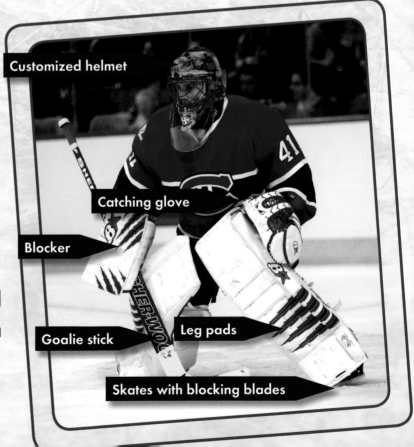

Customized helmet

Catching glove

Blocker

Goalie stick

Leg pads

Skates with blocking blades

Helmet

Face shield

Shoulder pads

Sweater

Gloves

Stick

Knee pads

Shin guards

Skates

27

SPORTS STATS

Here are some all-time career records for the Montreal Canadiens. All the stats are through the 2009–2010 season.

HOT SHOTS

GOALS

These players have scored the most career goals for the Canadiens.

PLAYER	GOALS
Maurice Richard	544
Guy Lafleur	518

PERFECT PASSERS

ASSISTS

These players have the most career assists on the team.

PLAYER	ASSISTS
Guy Lafleur	728
Jean Beliveau	712

BIG SCORES!

POINTS

These players have the most points, a combination of goals and assists.

PLAYER	POINTS
Guy Lafleur	1,246
Jean Beliveau	1,219

SUPER SAVERS

GOALS AGAINST AVERAGE

These Montreal goalies have allowed the fewest goals per game in their career.

PLAYER	GAA
George Hainsworth	1.78
Jacques Plante	2.23

PLAYER POSITIVE

CAREER PLUS-MINUS

These players have the best **plus-minus** in Canadiens history.

PLAYER	PLUS-MINUS
Larry Robinson	+700
Serge Savard	+492

FROM THE BENCH

COACHES

These coaches have the most wins in Canadiens history.

COACH	WINS
Toe Blake	500
Dick Irvin	431

GLOSSARY

arena an indoor place for sports

assist a play that gives the puck to the player who scores a goal

center a hockey position at the middle of the forward, offensive line

defenseman a player who takes a position closest to his own goal, to keep the puck out

goalie the goaltender, whose job is to keep pucks out of the net

Hockey Hall of Fame located in Toronto, Ontario, this museum honors the greatest players in the sport's history

plus-minus a player gets a plus one for being on the ice when their team scores a goal, and a minus one when the other team scores a goal; the total of these pluses and minuses creates this stat. The better players always have high plus ratings

points a team gets two points for every game they win and one point for every game they tie; a player gets a point for every goal he scores and another point for every assist

puck the hard, frozen rubber disk used when playing hockey

rivals teams that play each other often and with great intensity

rookie a player in his first season in a pro league

Stanley Cup the trophy awarded each year to the winner of the National Hockey League championship

sweater the name for a hockey player's jersey or shirt

wing a hockey position on the outside left or right of the forward line

FIND OUT MORE

BOOKS

Goodman, Michael. *Montreal Canadiens: History and Heroes*. Toronto: Saunders Book Co.: 2009.

Stubbs, Dave. *Our Game: The History of Hockey in Canada*. Montreal: Lobster Press, 2006.

Thomas, Kelly, and John Kicksee. *Inside Hockey!: The Legends, Facts, and Feats that Made the Game*. Toronto: Maple Leaf Press, 2008.

WEB SITES

Visit our Web page for links about the Montreal Canadiens and other pro hockey teams.

childsworld.com/links

Note to Parents, Teachers, and Librarians: We routinely verify our Web links to make sure they are safe, active sites—so encourage your readers to check them out!

31

INDEX

ABOUT THE AUTHOR

Craig Zeichner has been going to hockey games since he was 11 years old. He roots for the New York Rangers but likes the Red Wings, too. Craig grew up playing roller hockey in Brooklyn, NY.